TOLSTOY KILLED ANNA KARENINA

DARA BARROIS/DIXON

Tolstoy Killed
Anna Karenina

WAVE BOOKS

SEATTLE AND

NEW YORK

Published by Wave Books

www.wavepoetry.com

Copyright © 2022 by Dara Wier

All rights reserved

Wave Books titles are distributed to the trade by

Consortium Book Sales and Distribution

Phone: 800-283-3572 / SAN 631-760X

Library of Congress Cataloging-in-Publication Data

Names: Barrois/Dixon, Dara, 1949– author.

Title: Tolstoy killed Anna Karenina / Dara Barrois/Dixon.

Description: First edition. | Seattle : Wave Books, [2022]

Identifiers: LCCN 2021042899 | ISBN 9781950268535 (hardcover)

ISBN 9781950268528 (paperback)

Subjects: LCGFT: Poetry.

Classification: LCC PS3573.I357 T65 2022 | DDC 811/.54—dc23/eng/20211006

LC record available at https://lccn.loc.gov/2021042899

Designed by Crisis

Printed in the United States of America

9 8 7 6 5 4 3 2 1

First Edition

Wave Books 097

'What a terrible death!' said some gentleman as he passed them. **(AK 64)**

CONTENTS

Part One

If You Are Lucky

3

Being Nervous Is Only Human

6

Credits

8

Sunset's Sex

15

Comes

16

Where Inanimate Objects Have the Sturdiness
of Intoxication Momentarily Evanesced

18

Telepathic Kinesis

21

Part Two

Things Art Can Do, Part One and Part Two

25

Simile for Its Own Sake

26

Perfect Imitation of Something Familiar

30

Thru

32

Capitalism

34

Waiting

36

During the Time You Are Deceased

41

A Few of the Crimes You've Committed against My Heart

43

Part Three

Wanderlust, Heartache, Nostalgia, Burning Desire

49

Trance of Sorrow

51

Dusty Rabbits in Cosmos Borders

55

I Feel Sorry for You Someone
Said to Me Over and Over Again

56

This Is What There Is

62

I Have a Little Extra Mercy

64

Tolstoy Killed Anna Karenina

66

Notes & Evidence

71

Acknowledgments

75

25 January 1851
I've fallen in love or imagine I have;
went to a party and lost my head.
Bought a horse which I don't need at all.

—Leo Tolstoy

Remember that I am thy creature; I ought to be
thy Adam, but I am rather the fallen angel,
whom thou drivest from joy for no misdeed.

—Mary Shelley

I sleep with thee, and wake with thee,
And yet thou art not there

—John Clare

Part One

IF YOU ARE LUCKY

The same person will fall in love with you
over & over & over & over again & again

if you are lucky, if your luck holds out
over & over the same one will fall out of love with you

in order to fall back in
it is an excruciating process nonetheless it is necessary

you will need to be prepared to recognize
someone's love for you

as well as be prepared to follow it
as it wanes and waxes

unfortunately this means you will need to endure
long stretches without love

& these you will need to endure with patience and grace
in order to be prepared for love when it comes

and love when it disappears
with the strength you've gained

because you've read poems
and novels and stories

and you've watched movies
and looked at pictures

and you've lived with animals
and you've loved them

and by virtue of all these things
you've practiced feeling something

as complicating as love without end
and as complicating as love no more

you will have kept up in practice
you will be able to take what love throws your way

because stories and poems have wrung
your heart and shattered your brain

over and over again to watch you change
so now you are ready

so when Wednesdays that will never end come
& the necessary days without nights

try not to think of them
they will destroy you

the bright days with no love
the short days days without end

for those days be glad
as patient as a glacier

or one big starving panther
waiting for its prey

every time love comes
you will stand there

and stand it
or it will come again no more

BEING NERVOUS IS ONLY HUMAN

You might be a chipped-off edge
of an eggfly butterfly's wing tip

tilted in the left-hand corner
of a cracked aquarium

sitting behind a rusted dumpster
behind an all-night 7-Eleven

in an otherwise empty dim-lit parking lot
and it feels all right

without your wing tip's eye spots
you might be eaten alive

without your natural-born
elements of deception

it is necessary to search
for extraterrestrial intelligence

any other place we don't call *ours*
a place we can use to keep us alive

a place we won't recognize
otherwise, same story, so what

being nervous is one way to pass the time
everyone always says they can't tell

when one another's nerves show
everyone knows to affirm a condition

residing as it does mere centimeters
from prostration—to affirm

its existence is forbidden
we know everyone's intention

amounts to being kind
and we admit

these results
in far better circumstances all the time

CREDITS

And this creature of love I took from poems
I found in a book on the floor of a closet

I took their shapes and the smell of cedar
and I took comfort in how they looked at me

I took what I could take
from a Sappho of my own feelings

and this cold stare I took from her friend
Shakespeare

who I found to be also a friend always with words
to spare it is said he used over 12,899 of them

I took obedience to the turn of the earth
its seasons, its weathers

and time from Duchamp & possibly his sister
while the river I grew up with took me

to this sharp little *the* with someone
asleep under an overpass

and this *a* I took also from someone
I ought to have treated otherwise

I borrowed this *nipple*
from my own mother

who disowned me and chose never
to suckle me nor any of her children

neither sons nor daughters
a tender heart I took

from John Keats
and I took the souls of animals from John Clare

and from Mary Shelley I took to understand
a creator's responsibility to what she creates

I took to understand what's created
ought to be loved not abandoned

all along I took what I could
and I gave it away

for love and out of fear of loathing
which I took from all the holy books

and from Christopher Smart I took courage
to kneel down naked and be laughed at for it

I took from friends and lovers
all I could

without taking too much
all along to be rightly indebted

so if anyone chooses to feel what I did
they can rightly deny me

I took this into my heart
and while I did not always live up

to what I would have been had I been better
I took more from them than anyone

should take from anyone
what Walt Whitman could not give me

I took from Emily Dickinson
from her I took a slice of brain

at full operating speed and I took also
a sliver of her bedroom's wallpaper

I took from Marianne Moore love for precision
fierce humility before evidence

patience before conclusion
and from her friend Elizabeth Bishop

I took an understanding of an inability
to withstand living

I took hands half in suds from her
and did not give them back

furthermore I took fear
of our reasoning minds

from E. A. Poe which fear
I further found a mind's reasons

will stop at nothing
to fulfill its wishes

this bundle of nerves I found
among ratiocinations he thoughtfully presented

in order to give me what reason
could not accomplish

poetry could contain
and from John Donne I took an attitude

it turns out I might have fared better without
& from William James I took the dawning

of the significance of self-consciousness
as a boy's father screams

as his son leaves his life behind
while his son's brother listens

and thinks how perfect
his father's agony is

from Gertrude Stein I took comfort
in her audacity to love her writing

& as one way to spend her time
as I as a child took from e. e. cummings

dooms of love & words involved
with one another's personalities

I took what I could when I could take it
I took what I wanted when I needed it

I took more than I should have taken
and returned none of it

other times I took my share
when I knew what I took no one else wanted

I took more than I deserved
at least that's what I was sometimes told

I took what I could where I could find it
I took time when time offered itself to me

I took a look and I backed off
or I settled in

I took cover more often
than I should have needed to

I took a long time to understand
how much power lies in

giving and taking a life
all the while judging its value

it took some time before I found
what Flaubert does to Emma Bovary

no different from what Tolstoy
does to Anna Karenina

what I left I could not have taken
I left it for others for their own sakes

I took without asking
when I understood asking would get me nowhere

I took to whispers and secrets
I took to hiding in the folds of shadows

I took to it the way a newborn camel
takes to its mother's side

SUNSET'S SEX

It always spreads itself across the sky
as if it belongs there & nowhere else

it reiterates what the horizon wants
before the horizon shows itself wanting

it makes want happen
to want to be satisfied

it lays down everything it is
in order to be everywhere

it wants so it waits
it waits while it gives it

gives as it takes while time dissolves
and matter is no longer of concern

what is of concern goes without saying
without saying

desire is given
desire is sometimes water

COMES

little penis penis penis penis penis penis penis
the only way to make it more

than so little, brave and small
did I say brave

as to be barely there
is to make it repeat itself repeat itself the

one & the same the same the same
the only way to keep it where it goes

to understand understand understand
is to let it let it let it

scent the room with its essence
some summaries of thoughts ever after

every thought ever thought
by everyone ever thinking

this super huge giant super realized offering
just as that first wet bit

tiny opalescent drop
of near ejaculation

can seem as if some fabulous new life
is about to announce its arrival

WHERE INANIMATE OBJECTS HAVE THE STURDINESS OF INTOXICATION MOMENTARILY EVANESCED

It is understandable
to despise narrative

as much as it is understandable to love it
and to be drawn along in its wake

to anticipate
and to feel as if

you are experiencing a life
simultaneously someone else's

and in the course of the story—
as the story goes on—

hard to resist it
it becomes part of your own story

how else to experience someone else's story—
it is as if you are simultaneously

a tiny bit ahead of yourself
and a tiny bit behind

as if time's usual constraints are gone
& a brief illusion of omniscience is near

its usual moving sidewalk assembly line is gone
as if simultaneity is near

someone else's thoughts
have taken up residence in your own

while your own have withdrawn
to make room for these ghosts

of someone else's life and death matters
and you can say with a new understanding

and with true feeling—because you read it in a book—
courage faltered in the face of self-doubt

sweetness suffered while it suffocated
under it some self-pity soured

as self-pity raged while rage tore
at so many hearts

whose torn hearts bled pity
whose pity excited glamor

and its beauty felt undeserved
we could not allow ourselves

a moment's joy
for fear of its absence

what if we elevated
all else beyond superstition

& mysterious life allowed
no cloak over anyone's broken spirit

TELEPATHIC KINESIS

The beautiful orphans
found themselves wandering

in forests of terrestrial magnification
an enormous oversized elk

an elk of epic proportions
a giant of an elk

followed their every footstep
they could hear the cracking

of underbrush as his huge hooves
hit dry wood & leaves

they could hear his breath
they heard the thunk

of his antlers against a tree trunk
as they climbed into an open window

of a shack they found wide-eyed
in a green peaceful clearing

near a sweet little running river's edge
the elk stepped up

onto the shack's little porch
where it didn't really fit

night fell, the moon rose
an owl flew over the water

Part Two

THINGS ART CAN DO, PART ONE AND PART TWO

This could be you
no longer who you were is what you are

who you are could be who this is
this is how it feels

being someone
elsewhere

in eternity
there is something infinite

about him she said
there is something infinite

there is
something definite

about you he said
there was nothing infinite

about him he was
finite like a simile

SIMILE FOR ITS OWN SAKE

like a ghost ship in space
something see-through

how the moon used to be
something impalpable

untouchable
or when you go to touch it

your hand goes through it
something haunted

it takes something haunted
to haunt you

like a lake
like a half a head of hair

it looks idyllic and holds deep dark secrets
it looks like it has a steady surface

to go right straight through
like bent and broken toes

like the last few turns of a spinning wheel
like a sponge dripping blood

like a tired horse
like a broken pillow

like steel-toed shoes
like a long sharp winding strand of strange hair

strange hair, hair that is strange
that comes from nowhere

like a two-toned baby rattle or rattlesnake
like coca-cola

like where you were born
like where you come from

like from where you get your looks
like from who you are

like chills
like chills curving over your skull

like as if
your skull is a horizon

like light on a wall you're trapped behind
like gravy

like the last sliver of light seen through
bars on a door

like the smell of a just sharpened pencil
like when you first set foot through the door

like where you hope to go next
like a thought branching into other thoughts

like a thought one can't stop
like a thought you want nothing to do with

like that thought finally put to rest
like putting a thought in its place

like taking a thought away from other thoughts
like not letting one kind of thought

overwhelm all others
like being swamped

like water
like water in the rain

like rain on your face
like tears and rain mixed up on your face

like your face all wet seeing it in a mirror
like why this is happening

like what can be done about it
like who's there to see it

like eyes left out in the rain
like all the quiet pathways

in the near silence of your brain
in your brain's way of being

like a trance you fell into long ago
like keeping your own head down

like being in your head not mine
like who you are willing to let in there

PERFECT IMITATION OF SOMETHING FAMILIAR

With some attention to Utopia for beginners
to fall into an endless void, as if

that's hard
I measured you

from beginning to end
the length of your consonants & vowels

your silent syllables
and your louder percussion section

last night's black & white sunset set me off
the way you have a way of shearing off

what's garish
yours always has been

an ear I've whispered into
and an eye I've held steady

in comes radiant energy
in a vibration society &

for example all those encounters
with truly gorgeous farmers

who carried their side blades like scepters
who ruled the worlds of the back roads

all along the big river
where once barges toiled

and wanton wagons purled
as geese followed its course

to cities where night fell
stars went off

there was no light
anywhere and then

it got darker
and darker

and darker
and darker

and darker
and darkest of all

THRU

When wind winds thru my brain
it whips up not one word

not one thought though this is not
the hour of my death yet

it still is
a microcosmic answer to the question

living cells persistently ask
who are you anyway

anyone I know
other than through the name I'm called

music I hear
along with words handed down

to know some of what
there is to know

without obligation apparently though
everywhere visible

it comes down to
without you

if I am to persist
I am to stay

without question
what wind does

as it whistles
through us

which it does
in order to stay what it is

CAPITALISM

It makes me feel about as low
as *asap* makes me feel

as if someone is warning me
a snake's in my path

only it's a pretty snake
I'm in need of to make my life whole

there are so many kinds of us
coming in various versions of ourselves

and one another
there is, for instance, a type whose

bold sense of entitlement
is bolstered by an unquestioned

innate sense of righteousness
heady combinations

something calling for constant comparison
something sometimes useful other times

blindingly obliterating to beauty grace
love empathy sympathy insight courage

insight courage humor love grace humor
wit foresight generosity love humor truth

empathy grace sympathy empathy sincerity
grace truth beauty with courage

adventuresomeness surprise love humor empathy
kindness withholding judgment love humor empathy

recklessness generosity love humor despair
understanding love humor empathy recklessness

love humor despair loving kindness love humor empathy
humor joy sympathy love kindness courage

WAITING

There was nothing else you ever did
waiting was all you'd ever done

you may have been the best waiter ever
since time began you probably were

you must have been created for this one purpose
you must have been made to wait

you had to be for you waited from day one
that day one which was when you began to live

that was the day you began waiting from
you waited for milk to drip from your mother's nipple

you waited for light to turn into darkness
and darkness to turn around & go back

to being light waiting for birds to fly
for birds' shadows to say how far away

thunder comes in from
for rivers to pass by

for what comes along on rivers to pass
you waited while little by little

you could let yourself be forgotten
anyone could forget all about you now

you could forget yourself
while you waited better & better

waiting all through the day and all night long
from day one and every day after

what you were doing always was waiting
waiting with every bit of yourself

was your way of being in the world
waiting for letters to materialize

for letters to turn themselves into words
for words to be with other words

for words to do with other words
what words do

in ways to bring sense to what had not
seemed so full of sense before

you waited for sense to mean something
it might be anything it might mean sense

just in that one way
it was just as it was in that one way

all the while you waited you took
sense in just as it was without asking

it to be something it wasn't
everything was shown to you by your being

there to be shown it
all the while to wait was what you knew

& to wait was what you were always going to be doing
there could be nothing else

to do now but to wait forever
for forever never wanted anything

but to be waited for
for forever and waiting might be one and the same

or they could be another's necessary other
without forever waiting might just be a bother

without waiting forever was not what it was
without waiting forever could have no previousness

about it while you waited waiting was your one way
of being alive

you could wait as long as anything ever took
to be waited for

could wait for what never wanted waiting
to happen on account of it being

when you waited you did it so slowly
almost no one could see you were waiting

or that what you were waiting for was always
more waiting

when you waited there was nothing else
you were really doing except waiting

when someone was going to die you were waiting
for it to happen

you knew what you were doing was waiting
for dying to be doing what it did

you could wait when no one was looking or
wait where it might seem impossible

to be waiting there
maybe some of your best waiting

was waiting with someone else
with someone else who was also waiting

then waiting might be something understood
to be waiting for for good reasons

when you waited best everything all things
waited so they were all everything waiting together

with no desire to ever end their endless waiting
without ever knowing what could be being waited for

DURING THE TIME YOU ARE DECEASED

During the time you are deceased
your ability to communicate

with the living will be inhibited
you will be unable to explain yourself

with the same emotional urgency you once did
you will only be detectable to animals

you once spent time with on a daily basis
your attitude toward others

who have not ceased to live
will undergo abrupt correction

those for whom you
previously held suspicion

will resolve some way or another
any skepticism you once held

will palpably lessen
your overall assessment will soften

your understanding of weakness
will multiply

you may recognize the dawning
of regrets

you will wish you had admitted
previously

until you begin living again
you will have improved

in all ways save one
no one will be afraid of you

no one will stroke your hair
or hold your gaze nobody will

A FEW OF THE CRIMES YOU'VE COMMITTED AGAINST MY HEART

Arson most of all arson
tongues of flame flare lick like and like

I like fire
and I like water & a good flaring

larceny a little bit of larceny
treason exquisitely executed

peppered with a few petty kickbacks
like in self-serve brain surgery

in and out same day service
in a bargain up kind of way

you committed fog against me
you committed horses

against me
you attacked me with hummingbirds

you ambushed me with iridescence
you scalped me with trees

you blindsided me with stars
you pushed me over the edge

with bumblebees
you broke into me with gills

me with lungs under my wings
with books you electrocuted me

with words you tore me to pieces
with wildfire you blinded me

with inferotemporal neurons
you swindled me

you strangled me with satellites
with time & distance you slayed me

you pepper-sprayed me with music
you took out my eyes so you

said to polish them up some
you stole my petticoat my pretty chemise

you over-salted me with blizzards
you committed rain against me

you committed sharks against me
with rivers and meadows and mountains

you lied to me
with canyons and fog-shrouded peaks

you hid ravens there to kidnap me
you burned me with songbirds

& nightfall & morning
you scalded me with flocks

you stole my tongue with tides
with all of this you set me down

Part Three

WANDERLUST, HEARTACHE, NOSTALGIA, BURNING DESIRE

There was a word I skipped like a stone
over a surface as still as a water's mirage

with each skip its momentum gained
until it slipped past into what's invisible

with not one backward glance where I seem to be left
I said bye word so long

I picked up another word and held it in my hand
it burned a hole straight through my palm

my word I said when it was done
I picked up another word, I brought to my ear

its volume so low it was hard to make out
much more than its tone

I stored this word where words are stored
I looked away when a word I wanted to ignore

said my name
a herd of words arrived at my door

I stood aside close to a glass hidden enough
to guess who they are

these words are strong
if I let them in it might mean the end

of my time as it is
while I'm first all alone

with all that there is
as when

leaves in steady breezes
appear similarly engaged

TRANCE OF SORROW

There is a trance of sorrow
you can will yourself into

though you might not think
you can accomplish it so smoothly

you would not think so if it weren't
allowed to contain you

if you weren't it would not
be able to keep you

this well of sorrow this tower of sorrow
this sad sad sad song

this trance of sorrow you let yourself be in
exists with one single purpose

to let you know it is as if you are unable
to extricate yourself from its mesmerizing solution

it is as simple as if it is flypaper
and you are its one and only fly

its rightfully designated victim
you are a looseleaf sheet of paper

with something important written on it
and it is on fire

you have let yourself into
the center of the labyrinth and there

is no blind ant there to lead you
the long hard way out of it

if it is an ocean we're talking about
sorrow that drowns you

and if it is a sequence of waves
stirred up by a cyclone

you are lost in your sorrow
it will not let go of you

you are immaterial and it is omnipresent
it is omniscient and everlasting

and if it is a solution
what do we make of its contents

if it is a liquid in which you are suspended
what are the names of its components

what is it suspended in your sorrow solution
extricate solution component mesmerization

if it is a well you've fallen down into it
would there be a curious dog or

a kind-hearted donkey
to come to your rescue

you need a friend to notice
how deep into your well of sorrow you've fallen

you need a friend who isn't afraid
of all the no trespassing signs you've left behind

on your way down one after the other after
you descend as if they are crumbs

meant to be followed
you need a friend fierce and fearless, unafraid

to endure your anger flailing fighting
insults stubborn insistence crying

there is no way out and if there were
there would be nowhere to go from here

in your own well of sorrow you wish to stay
right where you are

as if you are trapped in quicksand
in your own mind

and your free will is gone
there is a force field of impenetrable

inescapable power
there is no way out you can see

if someone were to beg you
step back come again into another world

into thin air unintended to stop you
from living and breathing all the better

for having understood how fragile we are
when a trance of sorrow overcomes us

At dusk they grow ecclesiastical and sarcastic
though they never say a word

it is their posture
that judges us to be less than

the serene beings we are
they stare off into something

we will always miss, us
with our big brains and long nerves

and red scarves
they write nothing down

what they know is too profound
and they are good and true and

beautiful and
young

I FEEL SORRY FOR YOU SOMEONE SAID
TO ME OVER AND OVER AGAIN

If you keep saying to someone you feel sorry for them
what are you doing to them

what are you trying to do to them
what do you think you are doing

and if someone says no there's no need to feel sorry for me
someone says no don't say you feel sorry for me

and you say it again this time fiercely as if without compassion
without the compassion you believed you were attempting

to show them but had not done a very good job portraying it
or maybe it wasn't compassion and that's why it failed

but your right is to say about and to someone whatever it is
you like what is it then when it's transformed

into another kind of thing
maybe a good old-fashioned weapon of words

a weapon of spirit & mind destruction
I feel sorry for you

you might as well have said look what is wrong with you
can't you hear me saying I feel sorry for you

which could mean hey you I'm saying to you there's something
I choose to feel sorry for

who do you think you are to tell me not to feel sorry for you
and when once more I say no there's no reason to feel sorry

for me you say it again but I feel sorry for you you say
as if I didn't understand it the other times

but I feel sorry for you you say
what is this insistence you fail to take into consideration

and when I say no don't feel sorry for me
and you say but I do I do I do feel sorry for you

are you saying how grateful I should be
to have someone such as yourself saying to me

you feel sorry for me
and you say it again oh and again I feel sorry for you

and I say no there's nothing to feel sorry for me about
I say stop don't say you feel sorry for me

I want to say look I don't want your sorrow
you can keep it keep it for yourself for when you need it

and leave me be if someone needs to feel sorry for me
it will be me

and you say look it's important for me to say I feel
sorry for you

I need to feel sorry for you because
in that way I feel superior to you

and if I feel superior to you
I feel better about myself & all else maybe including you

I can say I care about you I can say my feeling sorry
for you is my kind of caring

I can say I must have empathy if I feel sorry for you
and I say no don't there's no need to feel sorry for me

and you say but I do I feel sorry for you
what are you doing and why is it impossible

to get past this impasse do you want me to look
at myself through your eyes

to look at myself with the pity you propose
would you like me to feel sorry for myself

would that improve this situation for you
do you pity those you say you feel sorry for

and what is the worth of your pity
your pity you put on me

for the sake of your pity's worth
how much can I count on your pity for

if I took it and let it rest on me
if I agreed for you to feel sorry for me

and for that maybe you might wish
I were to remain to be pitied maybe

for eternity would it be better were we
to feel sorry for one another

will you be okay if I say I feel sorry for you
can I say how sorry I feel for you

whenever you cross my mind
can my face awry my eyes conflate my head go slack

while I say to you I feel sorry for you all the time
each and every day

and when I do does our mutually inclusive
sorry for one another unite us or divide us

does it become a competition to see
which one of us feels sorry better sorry more

sorry stonger or truer or sorrier
and to be to be felt sorry for

what is that
to regret one's life

to regret I'm living
to help me see I am to be pitied

to have been found to be good for nothing
as far as you're concerned as far as you're concerned

I'm what you've liked to say something to fear
as if your fear holds on to you when

it no longer has me to feel sorry for
is that when what I am can be of use to you

to be good for nothing better
than for your pity to have a place to land

the sorry you say is a big bucket of water
you throw on me and then

I shake off what you've done to me
as if I were a big dog shaking off water

in one slow-motion motion
slow enough to look and to see

each single drop of water
all of a sudden each drop is its own

its own planet its own orbit
its own light over which

there is nothing
to be sorry for

THIS IS WHAT THERE IS

If you want to begin you have to go
all the way back

to where you never were
it is far to go there

nothing to pack
nothing to forget

nothing to remember
when you find yourself

thinking about your life
your very own tiny little one

& only real true life
and the life of eternity

be careful when you do that
when you find yourself saying

things to yourself such as
the universe

and all time seems at least 10,000 billion
years old

when you find yourself thinking
there has been there is there will be

try not to do it
when you find yourself thinking about

suns and moons and endless stars
and comets and rivers and valleys and mountains

one is zeroing in on you right this minute
don't do it it will turn you into a poet

I HAVE A LITTLE EXTRA MERCY

Do you want some
you can have some

within a whittled-down whisper
too smooth to be denied

I said sure a little mercy
has been said to go a long way

I'd be pleased
to have some

if you have some
to spare

so commenced my appearance
in several severed hearts

in the midst of the deep wide middle
near the pulse

of steaming hot heartbeats
meddled with mindscapes

strangely believing
mercy is not something

always in need
of being found

TOLSTOY KILLED ANNA KARENINA

a certain someone
knows something certain people
keep to themselves
certain enough to say *it's all mine*
it's not yours, it belongs to me
maybe it's no one's
—a wallet says I have money that's not yours
or a house says I have a place to sleep at night
or a coat says there's a body to keep warm
there's a certain time
a certain plant
a certain someone
a certain secret
a certain drug
certain terrible ways to end
a certain something takes place out of sight
it's important for you to picture it
in all its certain horror
unstoppable water, avaricious fire
someone throwing themselves under the wheels of a train
and what next
if I say I know a certain place

I claim a higher ground
because you don't know where
and I wonder why
if not to say I have something
you wish you had
a certain way I have
to cause you to want
something there's no way of knowing
what having it will do with you

Notes & Evidence
Acknowledgments

NOTES & EVIDENCE

Wherever found, AK passages from Oxford University Press World's Classics, ANNA KARENINA, Leo Tolstoy; Louise and Aylmer Maude, translators, Introduction by John Bayley, Oxford & New York, first published by OUP 1918, first issued, with a new Introduction, as a World's Classics paperback and simultaneously in a clothbound edition 1980 (excerpts from 11th printing of 1980 edition)

*

"Tolstoy Killed Anna Karenina" was written after reading about Joanne Kyger's journal and reading her poem "The Crystal in Tamalpais" and being reminded of a poem by Marnie Prange, "I Want What You Have"

*

Concerning the woman Tolstoy named Anna Karenina and what made her maker make her for obliteration, as fate and words pretend she kills herself rather than be her maker's victim, I'm thinking about what it means when someone calls something a tragedy when in fact it amounts to a crime

*

'What is the matter with you, Anna?' he asked when they had gone a few hundred yards.

'It's a bad omen,' she replied. **(AK 65)**

*

All it took, around 340,000 words, how casually we destroy one another

*

Don Francisco Goya named *the sleep of reason produces monsters* February 6, 1799

*

She wanted to fall half-way between the wheels of the front truck, which was drawing level with her, but the little red handbag which she began to take off her arm delayed her, and then it was too late . . .

. . . But she did not take her eyes off the wheels of the approaching second truck and . . . when the midway point between the wheels drew level, she threw away her red bag, and drawing her head down between her shoulders threw herself forward on her hands under the truck, and with a light movement as if preparing to rise again, immediately dropped on her knees. **(AK 760)**

*

I've always taken to heart Mary Shelley's FRANKENSTEIN; this sentence from Shelley's book serves as an epigraph for an earlier book of mine, BLUE FOR THE PLOUGH—*Remember that I am thy creature; I ought to be thy Adam, but I am rather the fallen angel, whom thou drivest from joy for no misdeed.*

*

"I Feel Sorry for You Someone Said to Me Over and Over Again" began as a conversation and ended later that night as an obligation to find its logical conclusion

*

"Trance of Sorrow" includes unspoken memories of an autobiography by St. Augustine and Mohandas Karamchand Gandhi's THE STORY OF MY EXPERIMENTS WITH TRUTH, *I searched here for God but failed to find Him.*

*

Just as in "Credits" I've left out so many animals, people, family, friends, places, books, schoolbooks, prayer books, library books, music, songs, weather systems, encounters, dreams, nightmares, accidents, coincidences, conversations, and so many other things of significance as to be distressed by my inability to pay due respect to the time and space this life of mine has taken

ACKNOWLEDGMENTS

American Poetry Review, Ashbery Home School, *Big Big Wednesday*, *b l u s h*, *Conduit*, *Hyperallergic*, *Iterant*, *jubilat*, *notnostrums*, *Plume*, Scram (for the chapbook *Thru*), *Volt* in which several of these poems appear

many thanks to editors and others who read and published some of these often in different versions and to Matthew Zapruder, Heidi Broadhead, Blyss Ervin, Catherine Bresner, Joshua Beckman, Charlie Wright, and Wave Books for unbroken encouragement; the ways words move from private to public come with precarity, disasters, and demons; endless thanks to friends, family, and strangers for forbearance and mercy

eternal gratitude to the Lannan Foundation for support of the most welcome and thoughtful kind, this book was finished thanks to their mission; Douglas Humble showed me welcome, leniency, and courage for which I am thankful

some who have either by example, friendship, kinship, or love paused my restless mind into a state of curious admiration and sometimes and oftentimes awe: my thanks continue for all time

THIS BOOK IS FOR EMILY AND GUY